FIRED UP!
Success

by ARIC BOSTICK

Fired Up! Success

©2013 Aric Bostick

www.AricBostick.com

1-888-629-0179

Aric Bostick Success Training, Inc.
1150 N. Loop 1604 W. Suite #108
San Antonio, TX 78248

Cover design and interior graphics by Düable Design & Development, LLC

Interior design by Brenda Hawkes

Author photos by Kathy Whittaker Photography

Printed in the United States of America

ISBN 10: 1490498168
ISBN 13: 978-1490498164
Library of Congress Control Number: 2013912050

*This book is dedicated to all those who think they have
lost their fire, but need to know it is still there.*

*This book is also dedicated to John Graeser—my confidant, my
godfather, my friend. The words written here are just bite-sized pieces
of the huge smorgasbord of wisdom you have graciously and selflessly
bestowed upon me. Without you in my life, I am nowhere.
Thank you with all my heart.*

Praise for Aric Bostick and FIRED UP!

Aric Bostick is a one-of-a-kind original. I saw Aric speak in Denver and he had the crowd on their feet and every person in the room was FIRED UP for more! I have recommended Aric's FIRED UP! keynotes, training events, and retreats to all of my clients. Books like this one will not only fire up your employees, but are guaranteed to engage and motivate corporate, government, education, and social sectors across the United States.

—Anne Bruce

Bestselling author of *Discover True North: A 4-Week Approach to Ignite Your Passion and Activate Your Potential* (McGraw-Hill), *Manager's Guide to Motivating Employees* (McGraw-Hill), and keynote presenter of *America's Got Talent in the Workplace!*

Getting Fired Up has given me the motivational inspiration to set positive goals for my work and personal life. It's given me the theme to use every day, think positive, let it go, and live every day to its fullest.

—Rhonda Benton
Southwestern Medical Center

I highly recommend any company needing to recharge and re-motivate their employees to bring in Aric! His high-energy presentation is packed with goal setting and team building ideas that all our managers are excited to take back and share with their teams. He is AWESOME!

—Lisa Watson
Human Resources, Marketing & IT Director
Cellular Plus

Contents

About the Author ix

Acknowledgments xi

Introduction xiii

Chapter 1—FUEL: What Fuels Your Tank? 1

Chapter 2—INVENTORY: Take Stock of Your Life 7

Chapter 3—REFRAME: Shift Your Perspective 11

Chapter 4—ENERGIZE: Exercise, Get R&R, Eat Well 17

Chapter 5—DECLARE: What's Your Mission? 23

Chapter 6—UNDERSTAND: Step into Someone Else's Shoes. . . .31

Chapter 7—PRESENT: Live Here and Now. 37

Conclusion 43

About the Author

Aric Bostick is a leading motivational speaker and success trainer who dispenses humor, wit, and heartfelt compassion to audiences from all walks of life. As a teen, Aric faced divorce, emotional neglect, instability, and abuse, but rather than surrender, he harnessed his energy to do something positive for himself and made real changes in his own life. As an adult, Aric uses his own experiences to guide and ignite audiences to succeed by overcoming their own personal stories, empowering themselves, and being a role model and mentor for others.

Kathy Whittaker Photography

Aric's audiences include students, teachers, and parents, as well as Fortune 500 Companies, leading healthcare and financial organizations, educational markets, and global business enterprises. Aric has inspired more than a half million people to believe in themselves and set higher goals by sparking their own performance and potential.

His latest book, *FIRED UP! Success*, passionately introduces energy and performance to the classroom and workplace by blending goodwill, inspiration, and highly practical tips from his world-class keynotes, presentations, and workshops. Aric is consistently a favorite speaker with corporations, associations, and schools. Visit **www.AricBostick.com**, or call 1-888-629-0179 today to learn how Aric can help your group become FIRED UP!

Acknowledgments

I want to thank my family, beginning with my father Jerry Bostick, who got me on the path of personal transformation at an early age; my mother Sue Isaac, who I love so much and has taught me so much; my brother Robbin Bostick, who has loved me unconditionally through all my ups and downs and provided me shelter and support when I needed it most; and my nephew Marty Bostick, who is my number one fan, and I am his.

Nancy, Mark, Haley, Gavin, Greg, Carla, Riley, Carson, Bennett, Tripper, Jennifer, Frank, Jack, Sam, Frankie, Reece, Whitney, and Christopher, thanks for being such great sisters, brothers, nieces, and nephews. I love you all so much!

Anne Bruce, thank you for seeing the light in me. You have given me so much inspiration. You are such an amazing woman, wife, mother, grandmother, and friend. Thank you for believing in me and giving me an opportunity to grow and expand and shine. Without your love, support, confidence, and constant reassurance, this book wouldn't have been written. Your input, contribution, and wisdom helped this book be what it is. YOU FIRE ME UP!

Phyllis Jask, thank you for your amazing energy, attitude, talent, and skill. I am blown away by how much better this book is because of you. You are FIRED UP!

Jocelyn Godfrey, thank you for jumping right in and helping us get this book done and making sure it was the absolute best it could be. Your help has been invaluable and I am so grateful you joined our team.

Susan O'Boyle, thank you for being my BFFEAE! Your unconditional friendship and ability to listen to me for countless hours as I blab about the minutia of my life have helped me change, grow, and become a better person. Our talks are the fruit of my life. They always leave me feeling better!

Mark Deleon (aka Maverick), my mentor, thank you for calling in sick to work, seeing me on television, writing down my website, and hiring me to speak to your Texas Teen Ambassadors. You changed my life forever. Our friendship and your mentorship have given me a life I only dreamed of. Keep making a difference in all the lives you touch.

E. Don Brown, thank you for believing in me and giving me an opportunity. You are such a great mentor and father figure and friend. Your wisdom and passion for kids inspires me to want to do even more.

Introduction

What does it mean to be FIRED UP? It means to be on FIRE for life—FIRED UP for what you *get to do*, and for *why* you do what you do.

The late great Philadelphia Flyer Hockey Coach Fred Shero famously said to his players, "Success is not the result of spontaneous combustion. You must first set yourself on fire!" I really believe that Shero is right. Many of us are not burned out—we are just not FIRED UP!

There are countless books, audio programs, and seminars out there all about finding your passion, and being happy and successful. Most are great and many can work for you. My own bookshelf is full of books—each of which I hoped would be *the one* to change my life. Each title felt like it had the answer to solve my problem at the moment. I would read bits and pieces and mine what I needed from each. I even subscribed to the motivational leaflet called *Bits and Pieces*, which offered short inspirational stories and quotes that made me feel good.

Don't Let Your Life's Desires Collect Dust

I would buy books that I leafed through in the bookstore only to have them collect dust on my nightstand—haven't we all done this? I would carry these books around with me, hoping that the words would leap from the pages into my psyche and change my emotional wellbeing. But they were all missing that special something that could really inspire me—something that could really make me feel FIRED UP to get out there and do something wonderful with the precious life I was living.

There are three key books I have read cover to cover that have changed my life and state of mind. *Return to Love* by Marianne Williamson, *The Untethered Soul: The Journey Beyond Yourself* by Michael A. Singer, and *WE: Understanding the Psychology of Romantic Love* by Robert A. Johnson. I carry the first two wherever I go and do my best never to forget what I learned in the third.

This book, *FIRED UP! Success*, is my personal philosophy, my very own seven-step strategy for tapping into your own inner joy, success, motivation, and most of all, happiness. My hope is that *FIRED UP! Success* will be the kind of book that you can refer to time and again to help transform how you feel and think. I want the *aha!* moments to flow from the pages into your brain and help you shift your attitude to one of joy and happiness, while inspiring you to take action immediately on your goals and dreams. I hope that you will refer to or quote this book when helping your friends, family, or colleagues through challenges. It is my hope that you will one day say, "This book changed my life!" I want you to tell your friends about what you learned and hopefully say, "You have to read this book!" Or better yet, "This book inspired me so much, I bought a copy for you!"

Wandering Outside Your Comfort Zone Can Be Tough

What I am describing here includes my hopes and dreams for you. Obviously, I do not have control over you or what will happen when you read this book. I have come to realize that many people really fear change. However, having said this, I also believe most people *feel a deep desire* to change; they just don't know how to go about it or perhaps may be too afraid of the unknown. Many of us want to talk about changing, think about changing, and dream about a life that is different than the one we are currently living. We want to rewrite our history. But rewriting history and creating real change takes time, work, and courage. And it's often uncomfortable. Change can be hard; change can be scary. Change often requires stepping into the great wide unknown. Wandering out of your comfort zone can be tough and quite difficult even in the best of circumstances.

I'll use myself as an example. I love to write and think I'm a pretty good writer. But I have a hard time disciplining myself to sit down long enough to do it! I have a ridiculously tight deadline for this book, and I procrastinated for the first two days! I am thinking to myself, *I am not sure if I can even pull it off.* It isn't fun for me being cooped up in a hotel room while life is happening all around me. Right now, I am speaking at the Ultimate Life Summit in Orlando, Florida, near Disney World. As I write this book, all I really want to do is get out there and talk, play, and laugh! But let's assume I didn't, because here you hold the finished product.

Instead, I realized that I needed to rethink my procrastination and negative and doubtful approach in order to get this book done—a scary endeavor!

I really had to look inward in order to get started. Why am I writing this book? Questioning "why" I do something is what motivates me most—and doing so leads me then to ask "what." What FUELS my fire to write this book? What really gets my motor running? Well, it comes back to accountability to myself. I want to write this book for me! I want to measure up and live my greater purpose. I have always believed I could write a book. I just never really tried before. I have something worthwhile to say and I want to put it out there. So here it goes.

Getting Fired Up Requires Evolution

I also have a greater purpose. I want to write this book to help others. I love FIRING UP my audiences. But then I go home. And so do they. The spoken word is powerful. But it is fleeting. I want to remind people about what I said and inspire everyone to take the actions I facilitate in my presentations. I want to give people the same tools and strategies I use and get them FIRED UP for a successful life! This book is a dream come true and helps me fulfill my life mission. In addition, I want to be a part of the evolution of the species. I realize that when I change and grow, and when you change and grow, the whole world changes for the better.

I love the life I have today because of the things I have done with the help of my mentors, counselors, life coaches, friends, family, other speakers, and authors. Sharing their wisdom and the steps they continue to pass on to me is a display of my appreciation to them and my way of paying it forward.

Why Should I Write This Book? What Is My Fuel?

Everywhere I spoke people kept asking me, "Have you written a book?" I would say no and make up an excuse like I haven't lived enough life yet, or I am too busy, or I can't sit still long enough to write a book. Here my audience was asking me for more and I was saying NO! They wanted to take the steps to success and I was too lazy to give them these principles in a format that could help them change their lives forever. These principles were passed on to me so freely through mentors and life experiences, and countless books, speakers, and teachers. Everyone deserves the gift of knowing how to create the life you really want and deserve and to overcoming any adversity that comes your way. I want this book to inspire others to get FIRED UP for their lives so they can pass on these strategies and become living examples of how much FIRE we all have within us. I don't *want* to write this book, I *have* to write this book. So here are the strategies that have changed my life forever. They have set me free! Now, do you think that I am too lazy and uninspired to get this book published on deadline? No way! Why? Because I found my FUEL!

Inventory Your Life—You Will Be Glad You Did

I am taking INVENTORY of what I have. I have 120 hours to write this book. That is 7,200 minutes! Okay, here's the mind shift: I have tons of time! I also have lots of love and support. I say to myself: I *am* a talented writer and speaker and I have a real gift for connecting people. I want to share this gift with others. Great musicians are compelled to play music, great athletes feel they must play ball, and great leaders are driven to lead. I want to share my enthusiasm. Therefore, I must write; I want to share my inspiration. I will shout it from the rooftops and I am driven to put it in print for all who want to get up and get going with their lives. I will do it for all those people whom I will never meet. This book must be written! Another minute wasted is blasphemy! Oh, and I do my best work under pressure. How about you? We all work differently and have different levels of energy and capacity to make great things happen. INVENTORY is what drives you to the end zone and beyond!

Escape Shame and Reframe the Way You Look at Life

So my next step in writing this book is I start working hard on REFRAMING my attitude. I think a little more about everything I am writing here in this introduction. I keep telling myself, I *know* I can do this! I say to myself, I *am* a great writer and I want to share my inspiration with everybody. This *is* going to be fun! In five days, the majority of the work will be done. The editors will polish it and make it all flow. I love writing. By putting the strategies of my speech into print, I *can* help countless others! I am excited to be an author. How cool does that sound: Aric Bostick, renowned speaker and best-selling author? WOO-HOO! I *can* do this! WOW! See how it works? Try it.

Get Energized and Declare Your Mission

I am starting to feel the critical ENERGY required to write this book. I can keep the flow of energy rising! It is 12:32 a.m. as I write this. I speak tomorrow to 150 students from around the world at the Ultimate Life Summit. I can't wait to share my journey and triumph with them. Talk about living your message! I think I should shower, or eat something, or go for a run, or just go to sleep and start tomorrow. But then I think, how many times have I said that? I'll start *tomorrow*. I'll exercise tomorrow. I'll call about that opportunity tomorrow. I'll study for my finals tomorrow. I'll end that relationship that is killing me tomorrow. I'll clean that closet tomorrow. No, I think, I must write this book—now! I will finish this introduction *tonight*. I have just refueled with some fruit and water and a two-hour power nap. One week of minimal sleep won't kill me. I am going to be fine for tomorrow! I must DECLARE it now—this book *will be finished in five days*! This is my mission. I will get this done! It's my declaration. What's yours?

Understand the Power of Touching Others—This Book Is for You

I UNDERSTAND who this book is for. It isn't just about me. It is about all the people who will be served after they take this book back to their work teams, family, or friends. It is for all of the people who don't believe that they can go on living a certain way. It's for all of you who want to change. You feel you have to change. You are FIRED UP! This book is for the cynical employee who thinks that his job doesn't make a difference and everyone else is to blame for why he is unhappy or why the company stinks. It's for the teenager who knows she can make a difference but has her life sucked out of her by the

Negative Nancys she might have to endure each day. It's for the tired and overstressed parent balancing work and family life. It's for you.

Difficulties Can Be Good
Who in this life doesn't juggle multiple roles—and sometimes drop a ball or two? This book is for you and all the difficulties you encounter: the teacher who has not seen a pay raise in years; has had his or her pension cut and benefits reduced; has no job security; has little support from parents, bosses, and coworkers; and is expected to change lives and inspire students to want to learn, but with limited resources. It's for the teenager who was abused, the student with a learning disability, the single mom trying to learn a second language so that she can get a job and support her family to give them a better quality of life. It's for all of us who have suffered with anxiety or insecurity about not measuring up or being enough in some unique way. We messed up at work, bombed a test, lost an important file, had a fight with our partner; we are the black sheep of the family; we don't trust ourselves because of the mistakes we have made. Life is difficult. But difficulties can be good—showing us what we are made of and strengthening our character and our determination. Like Tom Hanks' character in *A League of Their Own* beautifully stated: "It's supposed to be hard. If it wasn't hard, everyone would do it. The hard is what makes it great."

But many people have really tough and unimaginable challenges. Sixty-nine days in a mine—that is difficult; 127 hours trapped under a boulder—that is truly difficult. Losing a limb, a child, a parent, a best friend—that is unimaginably difficult. Fighting cancer, going through a divorce, finding out your best friend betrayed you—that is difficult. Being abused in some way—any way—by someone you trusted—that is difficult. I have experienced difficult. So have you. Somehow, most of us have handled it. I know that I can handle it and I believe you can, too. Five days to write a book for the greater good of people who, just like me, have suffered and want to get over it? Yeah, I get it. I *get* to write this book!

Purpose Behind the Passion
All we have to do is be fully PRESENT. We need to live in the moment. Keep a good attitude and remember our purpose and passion—like I am remembering my purpose and passion behind

writing this book. What keeps me centered? One thing I do is Bikram yoga—that's yoga in a 106-degree room for 90 minutes. My yogi tells me just to breathe in and out and focus on that breath. I do, and I forget about the heat. I slow down, I get present, and all of a sudden my fears and anxieties vanish. So now, I must be present and breathe, and then this writing will get done and with greater ease. I tell myself, this is no big deal. I concentrate on just being in this moment and enjoying the process. I focus and think about who I am writing for and I stay in the moment. This will be a gift to so many if I just stay in the present moment and write from the heart and share my experience. I feel a peace wash over me. I am FIRED UP!

And that is how it works. It is that simple and sometimes that challenging. It is now 2:25 a.m. I still have to get up in five hours. But now I am inspired! I am FIRED UP!

Fired Up for Success!
There you have it. This is my personal and powerful process for getting FIRED UP! In the next seven chapters, I will share more experiences with you and give you tips, tools, and techniques that you, too, can use to get FIRED UP every day. I will be clear and concise: Do THIS and YOU WILL GET THAT! But *you* have to do it! This book will not change your life! It will be up to you to do the work and create the life you want. So decide now if this is going to be another book on your shelf collecting dust, or the beginning steps to taking action toward who you want to be. On the other side of this amazing process is the real you who you have always imagined.

One final thought. Fred Shero also said, "When you have bacon and eggs for breakfast, the chicken makes a contribution, but the pig makes a commitment."

DECIDE TODAY!

COMMIT NOW!

GET FIRED UP!

August 2013

Chapter 1

FUEL: What Fuels Your Tank?

The first step to getting FIRED UP is to figure out precisely what FIRES YOU UP! This can be challenging at times because we lose focus about what we want and how to get it.

I meet so many different people who are simply unclear about what they want. I believe when we solely focus on what we think we WANT, NEED, or DESIRE, we will come up short every time. How many times have you received the raise, earned the recognition, bought the new car, or gained the relationship and you were still unhappy and feeling empty? My experience is that our fuel does not come from an outside source or material thing—it comes from the very core of our being. If you want to find out what fuels you, you have to think outside of what you want for *you*.

You Can't Always Get What You Want but If You *Give*, You'll Get What You Need

What exactly do you want to give or contribute and why? When you figure this out, you'll begin to get excited, your creative energy will begin to flow, and you won't always be thinking about the outcome or some bottom line quota you are trying to meet. You will become on FIRE because of what you are going to *give*, not because of what you are going to *get*. The interesting thing is that when you start giving, you most certainly will start receiving, but that part won't matter as much to you. Your shift in focus is the beginning of your new change and growth! And that results in self-fulfillment! You may not get precisely what you *think* you want immediately, but something good will come eventually. You won't have that feeling of falling short because you'll have satisfaction from within yourself—a reward to yourself, in a sense.

Every wonderful thing in my life has come about from the question, "How can I serve?" Zig Ziglar told his readers, "You can get everything in life you want if you help enough other people get what they want." I think that's one powerful statement. I became a high school teacher and coach because I had a coach who made a difference in my life and I wanted to do the same for other young people. One of my students asked me to give a motivational speech at his church one Sunday evening. That church told another church and then another and before I knew it, I was being paid to speak on a regular basis. I got to do something I loved, something that served others, and something I happily would do for free—but being paid made it that much sweeter! I stumbled into this amazing new career and it was the end result of something *I never even knew I wanted*— I was riding the wave of inner fulfillment.

The New Sustainable Energy
You may be thinking to yourself, "What does this have to do with me being FIRED UP for my life, my school, my family, my job, my organization, my community, or my bottom line?" You may be trying to get your managers to be better leaders of your stores. You might be trying to increase your sales. You may be trying to make the team, make the grade, or get the scholarship. You may want your students to pay attention in class and perform well on their standardized tests. You may want your employees to show up on time and perform their jobs with a good attitude. You may be trying to help your kids improve and succeed in school.

The point is this: *What fuels your fire is WHAT you decide to give, WHY it's important for you to give it,* and *WHO you decide to be because of it!*

When you think of what you can give, then everything changes. When you change your thinking from being needy to believing you have something worthwhile to offer, people will be attracted to what you have to give. People will want to buy your products and your managers will be fired up to lead their teams because of all you give to them. Sales will increase because of your phenomenal service and all that you stand for. Your students will be so excited to listen to your lessons, turn their work in, and give you their best because you are giving your best instruction—and doing so from a thoughtful and inspired position. Your friends will notice the change in you when you tap into your inner confidence and practice being a good friend. Your boss or coworkers will notice your new and improved attitude. Your coach will notice your new commitment and put you into the games. Your family will notice your new positive parenting approach and they will be happier for it. People will follow your lead because you will be leading with a bigger purpose. People will know when you are fired up because your passion and energy will become a raging WILD FIRE! Bruce Springsteen sang it best: "You can't start a fire without a spark!" *You* are the spark.

Wikipedia says that "the positive effects of fire include *stimulating growth* and maintaining various ecological systems. Fire has been used by humans for cooking, generating heat, signaling, and *propulsion purposes*." Fire is part of the evolution of the species and it will take hold of you if you start it! You can't help but to spread it to all those you touch! So my message is this: If you want to change your company, or your schools, or the lives around you, then start by *changing yourself*. Find out what you want to give that could start a fire of enthusiasm and passion to stimulate growth in your world and propel you toward what you really, really want! When you are whole and complete, you have so much to offer. Your company, too, has so much to offer, as does your organization, your school, your students, your family, your friends, and your colleagues. How can you better serve those around you?

Your Gift to the World Is to Serve
The philosophy of service fuels the biggest and most successful companies and people in the world. Simon Sinek outlines in his powerful book, *Start with Why: How Great Leaders Inspire Everyone to Take Action*, how Apple and Southwest Airlines revolutionized their markets due to their desire to serve the greater good. Apple wanted to level the business playing field by making computers that were affordable and easy to use by everybody. Southwest Airlines wanted to make travel affordable for everyone. These are now two of the most profitable companies in their industries. These companies don't just make computers or fly airplanes. They FIRE US UP! *That is their gift*!

3

People who love Apple products are so passionate about them that they're willing to camp outside for days—on sidewalks!—to be the first ones to get anything new from Apple. If you have ever been on a Southwest Airlines flight, you know the flight attendants are ON FIRE! They serve you with a smile, they joke over the intercom, they make flying fun—they sure inspire me to want to fly more.

Now it is your turn, your life, and your world. What do you want to give to the world? Let me be clear. I am not saying that you should not want any compensation or fair exchange for your values and services. I don't want you to live in a shack and be a martyr any more than I want to be a motivational speaker living in a van down by the river (as Chris Farley's *Saturday Night Live* character Matt Foley used to say).

Apple and Southwest Airlines are billion dollar companies. They serve the world, create innovations and services that serve us all, and are abundant and prosperous. What I am clearly stating is this: What gifts do you want to give the world? Why is using those gifts important to you? Because having a good attitude affects everyone around you. By identifying the gifts you have to share and being committed to make a difference in yourself, you will affect those around you. Envision the parent you want to be, then see your family dynamics improve. See yourself making a change at your school by starting an anti-bullying campaign or initiating a diversity appreciation week, and see what good things transpire as a result. Your attitude affects everyone you work with, work for, and interact with all day long. Practice being fired up by being kind to the clerk at the convenience store and watch how much fun you have!

Again, I'll use myself as an example: My fire is fueled by motivating and inspiring people through my speaking career and daily living. I want to help set people free from the chains of being less than the best version of who they are—and inspire them to do what they love and share their gifts with others through whatever it is that they are doing. I want to FIRE UP people to be the absolute best they can be! Are you unhappy with your current situation? Then change your mind-set to being the consummate best at whatever you do, to giving as much as you possibly can—whether you are a janitor or a CEO or a student. Put your best foot forward in all your efforts and wear a smile like a uniform!

Why is this so important to me and why am I sharing this with you? I really enjoy and treasure my life today. I want you to enjoy and treasure your life, too! I want to share the tools in this book for living FIRED UP, and explain the principle behind the message. That's my gift to you.

Now what is your gift to the world?

FIRED UP and Doing Something About It! Step #1

1. What is your gift to the world? What do you love to do? What are you passionate about? List your talents and all that you want to do with them. How can you use your talents to bridge the gap of where you are now to where you want to be?

   _____

   _____

   _____

   _____

   _____

2. Why should you give this gift to all those you would give it to?

   _____

   _____

   _____

   _____

   _____

3. Who and what would be served by your gift?

_____

_____

_____

_____

_____

Chapter 2
INVENTORY: Take Stock of Your Life

WOO-HOO! Outstanding job! Now that you know what FUELS you, let's figure out what is holding you back! For me, FEAR and RESENTMENT were the number one blocks in my life. Sometimes a tornado of fears would swirl in my head—economic insecurity, rejection, never meeting that special someone, losing a job, getting fired, not having kids, not being loved back by my family and friends—and hold me in near paralysis. I would play out the scene in my head of all the negative things that could happen or what I would feel if these things happened. But then I started to imagine the consequences if I did not try to fulfill my dreams and goals. What if I didn't get over this fear of rejection and ask for a date? What if I never overcame this need for constant love and approval? What if I never tried to become a full-time speaker? The list could go on forever.

I also gave a nod to my fears. What if my worst case scenario came true? Would I still be okay being me if I lost that job? Never met that special someone? Yes. Would I be a little sad? Probably. Would I make a determination to overcome those feelings and move along with my life? Absolutely. Sometimes facing your fears head on is exactly what you need to do in order to unchain yourself from fear itself.

Look in the Mirror
Being human can be tough. There are reasons why many people overeat, abuse alcohol and drugs, stay in toxic relationships, work insane hours, watch hours of television or movies, cut themselves, have an eating disorder, contemplate suicide, fear being ostracized on social media, or spend countless hours procrastinating. The reason is often the *fear of change*. It is difficult and scary to take a hard look at your life and realize you don't like what you see. It is easier to distract

yourself with destructive behaviors and not face what is keeping you from being the best version of you. Our self-esteem is a fickle thing— we seem okay on the outside, but our insides are in turmoil. Many people either play it too safe or throw caution to the wind. It's those deep insecurities that hover over us like a monster in the night. It's up to us to shut the door on them and tell ourselves that we have the power to overcome our inner fears. How do we create the life we want and achieve our goals personally, professionally, physically, relationally, and beyond? I believe it's by facing our fears and resentments and ridding ourselves of the harmful and malignant thoughts that cloud our thinking and hold us back.

It's my experience that the solution to our problems always lies within us. We know we need to make changes, but we may be just too scared to do it. I believe everyone fears change at some level. We make excuses for ourselves or maybe deep down inside we secretly enjoy the drama. We don't even know what it would be like to live without carrying that security blanket of fear or resentment—those feelings are oftentimes so deeply ingrained in us.

Ditch the What Ifs

I've spent my entire life figuring out how to be happy. I call it the "I'll be happy when…" syndrome: I'll be happy when I have lots of friends, ace the test, get the promotion, get the raise, get recognized for my efforts, get into a relationship, get out of a relationship, and the list goes on. My "I'll be happy when…" list has looked something like this: I will be happy when Mom is happy, when Dad is proud of me, when my brother and I get along, when I stop getting picked on, when I am sixteen years old and can drive, when I graduate from high school and go to college, when I finish college, when I pay off my debt, when I get the right job, when my peers respect me, when I receive love and approval, when my talent is recognized, when I become a full-time speaker and get paid to travel and speak, when I find the perfect mate who fits all of my criteria, when I get married, when I have kids, and on and on!

I don't know what's on your list. But I do know we all have fears, worries, resentments, and thoughts that hold us back. The good news is that's all they are—*thoughts*. You are not the embodiment of your fears, resentments, neurotic thoughts, or what you do or don't have. These are just thoughts to which we often give too much power. You may have had a bad experience but you don't have to give it the power to define who you choose to become.

Many of our wants and desires are actually based on lack of something and certain deficiencies we are experiencing. We let the *what ifs* shackle us to inaction: What if I only had better parents? What if I hadn't made that decision? What if they break up with me? What if I'd gone to college? What if I bomb the audition? What if that person didn't leave? What if I didn't get that disease? Maybe then I could be happy and all my problems would be solved. We think our past has damaged and scarred us in such a way that we can't move forward and enjoy our jobs, lives, and relationships. Change runs the risk of physical and mental challenges, failure, and possibly getting hurt. I don't know many people who openly embrace getting hurt. Do you?

Letting Go Sets You Free

I don't think I'm oversimplifying when I offer three words for handling the reasons why you are burned out, stressed out, and fearful: **LET IT GO!**

By letting go, you give yourself permission to stop wasting your precious energy on what hasn't been working for you. Why let these things keep us from success in the workplace, at home, and with our family and friends? LET IT GO now and GET FIRED UP!

How do we begin to make positive change? First, by letting go of those insecurities we hold dear. Then, by taking INVENTORY of our strengths. Are you FIRED UP and ready to DO SOMETHING ABOUT IT? Then keep reading…

FIRED UP and Doing Something About It! Step #2

1. Make a list of all your strengths on the lines below. This might be difficult at first. Enlist a friend to remind you of the value that others see in you. What makes you feel great about you? What are you good at? What do you love to do with passion? What would you do seven days a week if you could?

_____

_____

_____

_____

_____

2. What would you like to change about yourself? What fears, resentments, or habits have to go NOW so you can feel good about yourself? How will you face your fears? How will you confront and recognize the things that hold you back and make you less than your best? How will you grow your greater potential?

_____

_____

_____

_____

_____

3. Circle YES or NO—Are you ready to let this go today? Sign here, committing to begin this critical process:

Signature: _____

Date: _____

Congratulations! Picture me giving you a big HIGH FIVE! You are on your way and I look forward to being a part of your journey as you read on in Chapter 3.

Chapter 3

REFRAME: Shift Your Perspective

Whew! Don't you feel lighter? You have taken inventory of all your strengths. You've become more aware that you have many gifts to offer. Hopefully, you are now feeling freer from the chains of fear, resentment, and pain that have been holding you back. I am fully aware that letting go is a process. Your fears and resentments may sneak up on you again. I encourage you to keep letting them go. Keep journaling, going to counseling, or talking to friends—but no matter what, don't let fear and resentment stop you from moving forward.

The Wisdom of Bob Newhart

So how do we create this new mental habit? How does a person stop smoking, stop drinking, stop procrastinating, stop taking frustrations out on others, or simply stop running into the corner of the coffee table? We just STOP IT! There is a great *MAD TV* skit where famous TV icon Bob Newhart plays a therapist and Mo Collins plays a patient who fears being buried alive in a box. She shares how this fear is ruining her life. The therapist tells her, "I am going to tell you two words that I want you to take out of this office and incorporate into your life: STOP IT!"

The patient replies, "So what are you saying?" She continues, "I have had this fear since childhood!" The therapist interrupts her and says, "No, no! We don't go there! Just STOP IT!"

She shares other issues with him, and his constant advice is just simply to say, "STOP IT!" Sometimes we hate when the answer is that simple, *but it is*. Whatever you are doing now that is not working to better you, simply STOP IT!

I am not saying it is going to be easy. If you are dealing with addiction or major life issues, you most likely are going to have to seek help of some kind and surrender to your inability to stop it. But at the end of the day, you have to do your part. The behavior patterns, habits, or actions that are hurting you must be stopped and replaced with new habits or actions that are positive and move you toward who you want to be and where you want to go.

Adopting Your New Attitude
Now that we have changed what we do, we have to change how we think. I have heard that a miracle is just a change in perception. We have to see things differently. We have to REFRAME our attitude. I have used this concept in every area of my life. For example, without the difficulties I faced in childhood, I wouldn't have learned how to change and grow as a person at such a young age. My journey toward self-discovery started early because if I didn't start it, who knows where I might have ended up. My father's recovery from alcoholism was an inspiration and led him to become dedicated to personal growth. He would take me with him to motivational seminars and workshops and share his books with me. I was reading Zig Ziglar's *See You at the Top* as a freshman in high school! And look where I am today. I get to share what I learned and have successfully implemented into my life with people from around the world. Are you ready for a new perspective? Your journey begins when you take that mental leap!

The Tough Situation You Live in Doesn't Have to Live in You
Everything that happened *to* me has happened *for* me—I used my personal experiences as a youth to become a compassionate adult. Having experienced the awkward teenage years with divorced parents, a blended family, acne, braces, no girlfriend throughout high school, and countless other challenges helped me to understand the people to whom I speak and what they are up against. I can love them unconditionally and give them encouragement and hope that the hardships of their life will pass. I wouldn't change a thing from my past now. There's a quote I often use in my presentations: "The tough situation you live in doesn't have to live in you!"

You can REFRAME whatever situation you live in. As a motivational speaker, I often have to reframe my perspective. Most people see the happy, FIRED UP me on stage. But they have no idea I've endured airport parking and security, plane delays, lost luggage, and long walks to rental cars in rain, snow, and heat just to get there. Then there's finding the hotel, finding the location of the event, racing from the event back to the airport to catch yet another plane to do it all over again.

But I will never complain about it. NOT ANYMORE! My new perspective is, "I don't have to speak all over the world; I *get* to!" I used to complain about all my frequent travel and how I couldn't meet anyone because I was always gone. I would never have met all the amazing students, educators, parents, and fired up employees I call friends today. I see how much fun I can have at all the different places I go. I have a friend in the industry who says, "I love traveling and I haven't bought shampoo or lotion in years!" I now tell people, "I have the privilege of seeing the country and getting paid to do it and I have a never ending supply of little peanut snacks!" I think about how I would have never gone to Crawford, Nebraska. But I am glad and thankful I did. The person who hired me there became my best friend in the world.

Do You Want to Be Happy?

Every life has its good points and its not-so-good points. So does every family, friend, coworker, exercise routine, diet, city, and state. But when we can change our perspective and reframe it, *we take control of how we view the world* and life gets a whole lot better really fast. As I said earlier, I am currently speaking at the Ultimate Life Summit in Orlando, Florida. I am staying at a five-star resort and I get to go to Disney World every day. One of the attendees is from Colombia, South America, and I heard him tell another attendee how much he is enjoying having reliable running water this week.

Running water as a luxury? That changed my perspective in a hurry! The more mind-blowing thing is that he loves his country with an intensity I have never seen here in America. When I'm on stage and ask, "Where are my Colombians?" they cheer and dance like they won the lottery. They have no running water in parts of their country and they are cheering for how proud they are to be from there! They love what they have and appreciate what they don't have. How's that for a positive outlook on life?

One of my favorite books, *The Untethered Soul* by Michael A. Singer, which I mentioned in this book's introduction, has a chapter titled "The Path to Unconditional Happiness." Singer says that you really only have one choice in life: "Do you want to be happy or do you not want to be happy? It's that simple. Once you make that choice, your path through life becomes totally clear."

So do you want to be happy or not? Take a moment to RE-FRAME your life and your current situation and see how much better you feel. How much better could your life be if you chose to REFRAME things and adopt a new and healthier perspective, filled with greater appreciation and gratitude? My guess is that you would truly be FIRED UP!

Fired Up and Doing Something About It! Step #3

1. What are ways you can begin to see life differently? Individually REFRAME your education, career, relationships, parenting, health, hobbies, interests you haven't pursued yet but want to try, and so on. Build a new framework for every part of your life, then get ready to display it to others in your gallery of life.

2. List three of your major accomplishments. Make these things that you are particularly proud of. You may have finished a marathon, but come in last. So what? You finished! That's an accomplishment. Reflect on your personal and professional life or academic career, community service, recent events, or events from years past. Write about those experiences that fired you up. Re-live what you do so well.

_____

_____

_____

_____

_____

Bonus step: Instead of thinking about all the "to-do" lists in your daily life, why not start making "accomplishment lists" that take the burden of more to do off your shoulders and start lightening your load of responsibility with a sense of appreciation for how amazing you can be when put to the test?

3. Focus on and list three things, or more, that you LOVE about your life! Remember, the mundane can be powerful. Hearing your favorite song or getting a text from your BFF that makes you LOL can bring a smile to your face for hours. Watching your child sleep may give you great inner peace. People-watching at the airport can bring a smile to your face when you're stressed and hungry. Helping an elderly person who's struggling to get into a doorway at the doctor's office can make you feel like life's greatest hero. What you love about your life doesn't have to be huge, or about winning, or about flashy possessions.

_____

_____

_____

_____

_____

Chapter 4

ENERGIZE: Exercise, Get R&R, Eat Well

NEW ATTITUDES breed new energy! Have you ever looked at something differently and had the new perspective re-energize you? Our attitudes affect our energy! The question then becomes how do we keep our energy flowing on a daily basis? It also turns out that what we put into our bodies affects our attitudes and energy as well. It is very simple. To stay FIRED UP we have to put good fuel in our tank. I believe we have to think of our bodies like vehicles. We would not fill our cars with sugar. But we do it to ourselves every day. And we use loads of it! A 2011 United Press International article[1] reports the average American consumes 22.2 teaspoons of sugar daily, or about 355 calories worth of sugar. I am not saying we shouldn't ever have a cookie. But when we overdo it, we'll feel pretty crummy after the ups and downs of that sugar roller coaster.

Nothing Tastes as Good as Healthy Feels

It is recommended that we get the oil in our cars changed every 3,000 to 4,000 miles. Are you the type to wait until the check engine light comes on, or do you wait until smoke rises from under the hood of your car? It's awfully embarrassing to explain to the mechanic why you blew up your engine. Now instead of a $50 oil change, you are looking at replacing a $5,000 engine. We all know if we take care of ourselves each day, we won't break down and need an overhaul later. Have you ever waited until dinner to eat something and when you finally did, you ate everything in sight? I am not a nutritionist. I was raised by a Southern cook who fed me fried food and the best desserts imaginable. I didn't eat my first salad until I was 25 years old and my

[1]UPI.com, "Americans Eat 22 Teaspoons of Sugar a Day," *Health News*, April 30, 2011, www.upi.com/Health_News/2011/04/30/Americans-eat-22-teaspoons-of-sugar-a-day/UPI-35521304221808/.

first regular intake of fruit was shortly after that. It has been an evolution for me to learn to eat to live rather than live to eat. I know now that nothing tastes as good as healthy feels.

Garbage In, Garbage Out

What you put in your body matters. There's endless research that shows a balanced diet rich in fruits, vegetables, whole grains, and limited amounts of lean meats will help you keep your motor running for a longer time. I want to live a long time and I hope you do, too. I won't tell you what to eat or drink, but you know deep down inside that if you are sucking down sodas, eating junk food all day, or over-doing the alcohol, chances are you won't feel good. Did you know our bodies often disguise thirst for hunger? Drink as much water as you can. Water is the key to life and so good for your blood flow, skin, and energy. Stay hydrated and you will feel great!

Remember in Chapter 1 when I asked you to write about all the gifts you have to offer the world and your big reason WHY you want to share those gifts with others? We can't share our gifts if we are unhealthy or worse yet—no longer here. My dad jokes that he wants to die healthy! Nobody makes it out of this world alive. But there is no reason to suffer from poor health because you did not take care of yourself. Being unhealthy is often a choice—maybe not a conscious one, but a choice nonetheless. More importantly, we can't share our gifts and talents fully if we are operating with an empty tank. We certainly cannot state that we truly are FIRED UP if we are running on fumes.

Choose Health, Choose Abundance, Choose Peace of Mind

I am pretty adamant about this because I am living proof that good nutrition and regular exercise can transform your life. We must choose abundance and peace of mind if we want to have them in our lives. How we get there is something we figure out along the way. When I sought the help of a nutritionist and a physical trainer, and started doing Bikram yoga, my life and energy to live it changed for the better. I also started reading and watching movies about health and what is in our foods, and learned strategies for eating healthier at home and on the road. I simply started eating to live longer and feel good. I also noticed that when I eat and keep my health in mind, my moods stabilized, I felt more at peace, I needed less sleep, and I felt happier, more spontaneous, and more fun. The pleasant after effect was also that my waistline and stomach trimmed down! Everything about my life got better when I started putting foods in my body that supported my energy throughout the day.

Get Up, Get Going, Get Energized for Life!
We must move our bodies to generate energy. When a car sits unused for too long, often it won't crank up. We may hear it try but it just won't move. We have to drive it to keep the engine running regularly. The same goes with aircraft and boats. Therefore, the same goes for our bodies. We have to move our bodies! If you are serious about getting FIRED UP then FIRE UP your body and take it for a spin! Go for a walk, take a bike ride, run, do yoga, try Zumba classes, take up kick boxing, go to spin class, lift weights with a friend, or just walk around the block after dinner.

Your body is a magnificent machine. Make it work for you! Exercise for just 10 minutes and watch how much better you feel. Research shows that if you exercise 10 minutes, three times a day, it will give you the same benefit of exercising 30 minutes consecutively. Can you schedule 10 minutes a day? How about 30? How about an hour? The next time you are on the couch feeling exhausted or discouraged, get up and put on your workout clothes. Then go back and lie on the couch. See how quickly you get up and exercise. Not convinced yet? Try playing a song that energizes you and see how motivated you feel to get up and get going.

Or go to the gym and sit in the parking lot or just walk in the gym and look around. Chances are that in both cases you will find yourself feeling the urge just to get started. If you've taken the time to get there, you might as well go the distance and work out for 10 minutes…or 60! Half the challenge is just getting dressed to get going. So look like you are going to work out, and watch how the feelings will follow.

Get a Life—Relax and Unplug
Finally, rest, relax and have some fun! Get a life! What is your next

big thing? What are you up to? If your answer is the same old thing, you really may want to reconsider. It is recommended that people get seven to eight hours of sleep each night. I personally advocate also taking short power naps when you get the opportunity. Even 10 minutes of snooze time can ignite your enthusiasm. These practices are part of my energy maintenance plan. So schedule in your chill time just to sit back and unwind.

But I also want you to consider the ideas of RECHARGING and REDEDICATING yourself. What would recharge your battery? Do something that lifts you up spiritually, plugs you in mentally, and gets you going physically! Have you ever wanted to learn how to play the guitar? Learn French? Take ballroom dancing lessons? Master a new software program on your computer? What could you dedicate your-self to that would really get you excited? It's like putting new spark plugs in your engine. You will have a new fire within and you will look forward to doing this activity. It will also energize you because you will be up to something new. Your life is more than just a have-to-do. Having a new activity to look forward to will help light your inner fire!

Consider how much time you have spent relaxing by watching television. Did you feel better afterward? Maybe, but other times you may have felt worse. According to the A.C. Nielsen Co., the average American watches four hours of television a day. That is 28 hours a week, which translates into two months of non-stop television viewing! I have been that person! How about you? When I limited my viewing time, I got so much more done. But here's what's more important: I spend more time with my family and friends. I enjoy re-lating to others and being a part of the world more than I did watch-ing it go by on a TV screen.

Go on a Media/Techno Strike!
Do you ever unplug during the day? I'm talking about turning off your iPhone, iPad, iPod, and any other electronic devices you use regularly. Go on a media/technology strike for an hour or two and see how you spend your time. Maybe you can cook a nutritious meal for your family and eat it with them, minus the distractions! Or maybe you could have a conversation with the person sitting next to

you rather than texting someone miles away. The constant interruptions of pings and beeps can really derail your train of thought when you're trying to chill out and spend quality time with those you love and care about most. My friend and civility and performance expert Diana Damron calls cell phones "rectangular bullies." Are you being bullied by your cell phone or other electronic device? If yes, put a stop to the bullying now.

Do Something for the First Time Again
Finally, rededicate yourself to something you've always loved and enjoyed, but have stopped doing because you won't make the time. Play the piano, play a round of golf, plant a garden, meet your best friend for lunch, or take your child to the park. What activities did you enjoy in the past that you may have abandoned? Rededicate yourself to doing these things again. One of my favorite quotes is, "When is the last time you did something for the first time?" RECHARGE by starting something new. Do something for the first time, or REDEDICATE yourself to doing something you used to do—but now enjoy it as if it was the first time all over again!

Let's make a plan now for you to ENERGIZE yourself and get your candle burning bright again for years to come!

FIRED UP and Doing Something About It! Step #4

1. Avoid the energy sucks! This requires making a list of what you might be doing as a habit—things that suck the energy out of you and actually break down your body and make you feel bad about yourself. Then, channel your inner Bob Newhart therapist and STOP IT!

_____

_____

_____

_____

_____

2. Replace that old bad habit with a new good one. Create a list of what types of exercise and nutritional habits you can adopt that will support your long-term health and wellness. List the resources, including people who can coach you in the moment. I guarantee that this will help you with your plan of action and support you in your new life goals.

   _____

   _____

   _____

   _____

   _____

3. Declare a call to action now! Create a plan to recharge and re-dedicate yourself to things you have always wanted to try—or those things that you used to enjoy. Check the Internet for activities and events in your area. Next, think ahead. What can you experiment with and try that you have never tried before? Skydiving? Learning to play an instrument? Become fluent in a foreign language? Write your own book? Build a house? Dream big! What would you do if you knew you couldn't fail?

Chapter 5

DECLARE: What's Your Mission?

Now that we are fueled up, have taken inventory, have reframed our perspective, and have become energized, it is time to DECLARE and DECIDE what we will do and who we will become from this point forward. The power of our thoughts and words can literally move mountains—those enormous mountains of fear, disappointment, and lack of confidence that have been holding us back.

If You Declare It, It Will Come

The first real goal I ever set to paper was my desire to make the high school varsity basketball team as a sophomore. In the spring of my freshman year, our coach requested our goals for the next season. He asked, "What team do you WANT to make next season?" When someone asks what you want, that generally means you have a choice. I signed up for junior varsity to be on the same team as my friends. After writing our goals, we reviewed them with our coach one on one. It was in that meeting that Coach challenged me to try to make the varsity team. I knew of only one sophomore who had made varsity. His name was Brian and he worked harder than every one of us combined. He was determined to be the best player in our school and had a dream of playing college basketball. Coach believed I could achieve more and encouraged me to partner with Brian. I had to go for it!

I introduced myself to Brian and told him my goal. He graciously worked out with me. We invested our own time and money to attend summer basketball camps together. I really admired Brian. He had a burning desire to be the best he could be. He was not the fastest, the strongest, or the most graceful player on the team, but he was the best! All summer I followed his lead.

My skills improved but I still lacked confidence. I harbored doubts and feared failure, and at times it would really affect my game. My father had introduced me to the practice of affirmations a few years before, so I declared out loud every day, "I am a sophomore on the varsity basketball team!" I would say this hundreds of times a day, and really feel it to my core and in my bones. These affirmations began to sink into my subconscious. My confidence increased and I played more like a guy on the varsity team. I made the varsity team as a sophomore that season.

I have used this practice ever since. I set my goals on paper and then create an action plan to achieve those goals. Finally, I make a list of affirmations and say them out loud to instill in myself the belief that my dreams can come true. This practice has helped me focus on where I want to go and who I want to become. And now, even if I don't achieve my aspirations immediately, this practice gets me closer to my heart's desires.

Thoughts become Things

We are what we routinely say, think, and do. Thoughts do become things. I believe declarations motivate us to do what we need to do to bring about truths in our lives. *Webster's New World College Dictionary* states that to declare something is to make it clearly known, state, or announce openly and formally, and to reveal one's true character or identity. What do you declare? What is your truth about your life? What do you want to give, have, do, be, own, let go of, grow, or care for? Declare it! Make it specifically known—to yourself or to others— what it is that you want! At customs in the airport, we have to declare what goods we bring into a country when we travel. What are you going to bring into your life today? Well then, DECLARE IT!

What's on Your Five-Year Declaration List?

While at La Costa Resort in Southern California, I was browsing the gift shop and came across a particular book series—*The 5 Book*, *The 1 Book*, *The 7 Book*, and *The 2 Book*. (They can also be found at www.Live-Inspired.com.) Each book focuses on—you guessed it—a numeric theme that corresponds with a life ambition. I had been procrastinating on some of my personal and professional goals, like becoming an author, so I thought I'd find some inspiration within these books.

I couldn't decide which one to get, so I asked the young lady behind the counter to help me pick one. She said, "I would get *The 5 Book!*" *The 5 Book* challenges you to make a plan for the next five years of your life so they can be the best five years of your life. I asked if she owned it and she said, "No, I have two toddlers and can't afford it." I replied, "Well, how about if I buy a copy for me and a copy for you and I will autograph yours and you autograph mine, and we will read it, work the steps, and see where we are in five years?" She was ecstatic and touched. We exchanged contact info and signed each other's books.

Later that afternoon, I saw the same young lady as I was trying to find something healthy for lunch, and she said, "You should treat yourself to one of our delicious burger and shake combos! You are on vacation!" I replied, "In five years, I am going to be ripped. I will have the veggie wrap instead. My five years started today!" Your five years starts *the day you decide and DECLARE it*! Why not start today?

And here's the funny thing about finding that particular book at La Costa Resort of all places: La Costa is one of the pictures on my dream collage. A dream collage is a visual representation of your goals and dreams that gives you a focal point to shoot for in life; mine is literally a poster I created from magazine clippings and photos I've collected. For instance, if you dream about graduating with a doctorate from Columbia University, then you may have a photo on your dream collage that depicts a Columbia graduate dressed in a cap and gown holding a diploma on graduation day. You can find pictures regarding career goals, relationship goals, fitness goals, dream jobs, desired vacation destinations, dream cars, houses, pets, the list could go on forever. Visualization is easier when you find eye-catching examples of what you want and display them where you can absorb the ideas and attract the end results into your life. Life is like a buffet but you have to place your order! Have fun creating a dream collage of your FIRED UP LIFE!

FIRED UP and Doing Something About It! Step #5

1. Visualize where you want to be in five years and then describe your vision in detail.

   In five years, I will _____

   _____

   _____

   _____

   _____

   _____

2. Set a goal or two in the following areas, and feel free to add your own areas of focus. Be as specific as possible. At the end of each goal, write these words: "This or SOMETHING BETTER!"

   • Professional/Career Goal: _____

   _____

   _____

   _____

   • Educational/Self-Improvement Goal: _____

   _____

   _____

   _____

   • Personal Goal: _____

   _____

   _____

   _____

- Health Goal: _____

_____

_____

_____

- "Wouldn't it be cool!" Goal: _____

_____

_____

_____

3. Make an Action Plan. Write the specific steps you will take to turn these goals into accomplishments. When you do this, you breathe life into your plan. You give it depth and breadth. It's no longer just words on paper. It's experiential and alive.

- Professional/Career Action Plan: _____

_____

_____

_____

- Educational/Self-Improvement Action Plan: _____

_____

_____

_____

- Personal Action Plan: _____

_____

_____

_____

- Health Action Plan: _____

_____

_____

_____

- "Wouldn't it be cool!" Action Plan: _____

_____

_____

_____

4. Why NOT YOU? DECLARE it now! Write a personalized list of 10 affirmations and declarations you want to hear come out of your mouth every day. For example: I deserve good things in life! I am a good friend! I am so blessed! I am thankful for my good health! I am beautiful! I am worthy of receiving love! I can do this! I can lose weight! I will work out today! I will get healthy! I am grateful for my talents and abilities. I am so lucky! I am so fortunate! I have plenty of time! This is so much fun! I love being with you! What a great day I am having!

1. _____

2. _____

3. _____

4. _____

5. _____

6. _____

7. _____

8. _____

9. _____

10. _____

I want this to work for you! But only you can make it real. Make copies of your goals, declarations, and statements you desire to say all the time. Read them every morning, cut them up, put them on your wall at the office, on your bathroom mirror, and add them to your dream collage! The repetition of your affirmations draws them closer and closer to you, day after day.

5. Create a FIRED UP portrait of your FIRED UP LIFE! Look back at the goals you have written above and the steps you have taken in each of the previous chapters. Then make a list of all the things you want to see in your life and the things you want to let go of. Let your imagination go wild and have some fun!

There are even many wonderful and free collage apps out there, like Pic Collage, that can help you create your ultimate dream collage! Chunk down these areas and visualize your end results. What does it look like? What does it feel like? How does it smell? Where will you stand the day you achieve these results? What city will you be in? Who will be by your side? What will he or she represent to you?

Go to Google Images and type in the words on your list. Copy and paste pictures of what your FIRED UP LIFE will look and feel like. You can also use magazines or your creative ability to draw your dreams. You can add your declarations and quotes to this portrait as well. There is no wrong way to create your FIRED UP LIFE!

Put your portrait in a prominent place so you can see it often and feel the feeling of dreams already being accomplished!

Dream it. See it. And then be it!

Chapter 6

UNDERSTAND: Step into Someone Else's Shoes

Tremendous job! You are ROCKING now! I am so impressed with your willingness to transform your life and take the initial steps toward being the person you truly are. So the question is, why do all of this? This is a lot of work. The reason goes back to having that FUEL for your fire. One reason you may be doing all of this is so that you can really serve and connect with others. Now that you have declared who you want to be and are working toward the best version of you, it is time to look beyond yourself and realize how much you really can affect others in a positive way. You can spread the fire and fan the flame in all those with whom you meet or work.

I have had times in my life when I was so focused on myself and my situation, my happiness, my career, my life, and what I was trying to accomplish, that I lost focus on the big picture. Now I know that my entire career and life really is based on giving. The happiness in my relationships is based on giving. My health and wellness is based on giving my body what it needs so I feel good, and can be my best and give my best to others. When I am happy, I can contribute to others' happiness. I meet so many student leaders, youth educators, sales people, managers, and leaders of organizations. The people who seem to be the happiest and are usually having the most fun and making the biggest difference are the people focused on consistently giving more to those they serve.

They do the little things, like greet people with a smile and learn people's names. They write thank you notes and learn about the personal lives of those they serve and those with whom they work. Something as small as a written note can have the biggest impact on the person receiving it.

Service with a Smile (and Cookies and Milk)

Early in my career as a speaker, I witnessed the best illustration of this principle. I was hired to speak to 22 student leaders, called Texas Teen Ambassadors. Their job was to promote anti-smoking legislation and encourage their peers not to smoke or to quit smoking. Talk about giving to others! These kids were putting themselves out there for the good of others in a big way. I thought I was going the extra mile teaching these students what it meant to be a real leader. But then I met Kim, the waitress at our hotel.

The first night, the students and I ate in the hotel restaurant. Kim, a petite Asian woman, wore the biggest smile I had ever seen. She buzzed around throughout dinner taking care of us, and I saw how this lady was on FIRE for others. She treated the students as if they were highly paid executives. We asked for extra rolls and she ensured they were fresh out of the oven! She refilled our tea and water, and wore that same big smile while doing so. Our preordered meal included lemon pie for dessert, but Kim brought us a complimentary batch of hot chocolate chip cookies made especially for us! The students and I were FIRED UP!

I asked Kim about getting some milk to accompany our cookies. She told me that milk was normally $1.60 per person. I told her I would be happy to pay for the milk. She brought out a tray of milk and told us that the restaurant usually charges for milk, but that today it was FREE! We all cheered and clapped for Kim—and as we were leaving, I saw students hugging her and showing their gratitude. I was blown away!

Paying It Forward with Kindness

The power of kindness inspires others to display future acts of kindness.

Two days later, the student ambassador training ended. I was sharing my last words of wisdom with the students when the doors burst open and in walked Kim holding—you guessed it—a batch of hot cookies and cold milk. Kim received a standing ovation from the students! FOR COOKIES! When the room settled, I asked Kim to join me at the front of the room. I told her that it was my job to teach these students how to care about others, but that she truly demonstrated it with her actions, infectious smile, and heartfelt actions for us all. I asked her, "Would you share why you love your job so much? What inspires you to be so kind to us?"

She paused, smiled, and simply said, "It is my pleasure to serve you." Let that sink in. She gets pleasure from giving, and as she gives it, it returns to her in various ways. Some may say that is cultural or that it is just a trait within the hospitality industry. I think it's more than that.

Living the Golden Rule

No matter what life we lead, we are in the people business. When we make others feel important, appreciated, and recognized, and when we go the extra mile, we understand the true meaning of being FIRED UP! Being fired up is about UNDERSTANDING that your life, your job, your position, and your mission is about *serving others*. Some call it servant leadership. Think about it. How can you help someone if you don't understand and serve them?

Kim understood that these 22 students were without their families in a city far from home, staying in a hotel for perhaps the first time, and participating in leadership training all day. She knew intuitively that a big smile, lots of kindness, and nurturing—and of course cookies, like any great mom would bake for her kids—would make them feel welcome and at home. She didn't get paid to provide that. She said it herself: she received happiness from serving others. If you truly want to make a difference in your community, in your school, in your company, in your organization, with your co-workers, friends, and family, and with everyone else in your life, then put yourself in those people's shoes and consider how you might want to be treated. Then do those very things to create that service. I promise you most often the measure you give will be the measure you receive, be it appreciation, an improved relationship, an accolade, or a raise. How you feel about *you* will be the best reward.

Consider for one moment that the guy who cut you off in traffic might be late to work. If he didn't hit you, LET IT GO. Consider that the person answering your customer service call may be going through a divorce, fighting for her kids, or having a few personal challenges. Consider the co-worker whom you despise. He or she might have problems beyond your knowledge, and might need you to cut him or her a little slack so you both can get through the day in peace. Consider that the weird kid at school might be insecure about himself because his grandmother with dementia is living at his house and everyone at home is stressed out from helping to take care of her. Consider the teen mom who lives at home and faces the judgment of her peers and the whole of society daily. Consider the Golden Rule.

My point is that life is difficult enough without introducing hostility toward one another. We all have issues, challenges, and personality defects that make us a little nutty at times. I find that if I try to take another person's perspective before reacting, I have a better chance of relating and connecting, and often have a better outcome. Maya Angelou once said, "I've learned that people will forget what you said, people will forget what you did, but people will never forget how you made them feel." When you act with kindness, it's your gift to the world—and it makes the world of the person receiving your kindness a little bit brighter. Don't you want in on that?

Think about every grievance you have ever had. How often did you try to take in the other person's perspective before letting him or her have it? Every time I pause and think about the other person's point of view before I respond, things usually go smoothly. I have to think about what my assistant may be feeling or dealing with before I discuss what I want done. I have to think about my clients' perspective and expectations when preparing for their events. I have to consider what my parents are going through at this time of their lives and demonstrate patience and understanding. I have to do the same with my friends as well. When I come from that place of understanding, I feel peace and control.

As a result of implementing this in my life, I now view difficult situations, which used to bring out the worst in me, as opportunities to practice being my best. Who needs your understanding? Whose perspective do you need to better understand?

I can't guarantee that you will get a raise, move up the corporate ladder, get that internship, or get a pat on the back for doing any of these things. There will be times when people will treat you with love and give you the same understanding you give them, and there will be times when they won't. But I'm betting you will feel a whole lot better and cause a lot less damage if you take the high road of understanding and focus on being a good, kind, giving, and caring person. It is my experience that things usually go pretty well when I practice understanding—especially when I don't expect anything in return.

So keep your intentions in check. Work to UNDERSTAND, and you'll be FIRED UP!

FIRED UP and Doing Something About It! Step #6

1. Challenge yourself to smile at every person you come across today and reflect on the reaction you receive.

2. Learn the names of the people you interact and work with. Call them by name and see if you notice a difference in how the interactions go.

3. Make a list of people in your life that you are related to, work for, go to school with, or anyone in general with whom you regularly cross paths; or someone you are holding a grievance against or with whom you may be upset; and then hypothetically walk in these people's shoes. What might they be going through? Write about it. If you are led to call or speak to some of them, do so with understanding and kindness.

4. Write a note or make a call to anyone to whom you want to show appreciation, care, or concern. Apologize and ask forgiveness from those whom you have wronged. Understand that *what you do matters*, not just to yourself, but also to those around you. Be kind. It really does take a village to make the world a better, more FIRED UP place to live.

Chapter 7

PRESENT: Live Here and Now

Have you ever contemplated death? My favorite chapter of Michael A. Singer's book, *The Untethered Soul*, asks the reader to contemplate death. He states that, "Death is our greatest teacher." His words resonate with me. I am learning that if you want to know how to live, you should try thinking about your pending death. Life is so precious, yet we waste it by worrying, being afraid, being angry, procrastinating, watching countless hours of television and movies, or obsessing about our body's imperfections. We miss out on life because we waste it thinking about things we can't control or that don't even matter. We forget to live because we forget how easily we could die.

Take a moment now and contemplate your death.

Today **Is the Real Gift**

Now start worrying about something trivial like why your girlfriend hasn't returned your call or all the things on your to-do list. Which of these are really important? Think about dying tomorrow and then locate all your fears and resentments. Where are they now? Gone! Forgotten! Petty grievances fly away when you contemplate death. All we have is the present. Enjoy the PRESENT now. Be PRESENT in the moment and in everything you do. Get FIRED UP about it!

Do you want to waste another moment worrying about what happened yesterday? How much fun are you having when you worry about what might or might not happen tomorrow? If you were going to die today, would you spend all day writing emails, surfing the net, or reading Facebook updates? Would you read a tabloid magazine all day? Would you complain about the weather? Would you get upset at your child, your friend, your spouse, your parents, or your co-workers? How about that disgruntled customer? If today was your last day on earth, would you let a customer's petty grievance over a measly $2 get the best of you? NO! You might smile and laugh and gladly try to meet her needs by giving her two of your own dollars just to see how she reacts.

If you knew that today was your last day alive, what would you say to the people you love or work with—or those you serve at your work, school, or organization? Would you take the time to compliment them, or write them little notes of gratitude, or send them a quick text to let them know how much they mean to you? *What are you waiting for?* Why not start NOW?

Leave Your Soul Print

As I am writing this chapter, it is well past midnight. I have to meet my deadline. I'll have completed this book in five days! I couldn't have done it without a lot of help, though. My team is FIRED UP too! They are up late with me from coast to coast. My editors are on the East and West Coasts and they are working away. We have been writing and editing non-stop for three days to get this book done. Why is this so important to get done on time? I may not live to see tomorrow—who really knows?—and I want my truths in print and accessible to others who also want to be FIRED UP! My life has meaning and purpose and so does yours! I may be ashes tomorrow but my spirit will live on. My good friend and best-selling author and speaker Anne Bruce calls it leaving your soul print on earth. This book is part of my personal soul print. What's yours?

When you pass on and a loved one is sharing your eulogy, what would you hope they say about you? What will be your soul print? Just like a young child's handprint leaves an impression on a piece of paper, what impression will you have left behind? You make a difference just by your mere presence. How you show your FIRE to the world is important! Have fun, live life, laugh often, and make others feel special. How will you be remembered? Will people smile and laugh when telling stories about you? To leave a lasting soul print, your FIRE for life must be burned into the memory of all those you touch.

Sobering Consequences of Being Distracted

How do we stay in the present with all of the distractions we face in today's modern society? With televisions, computers, cell phones, iPods, and countless other gadgets and games distracting us 24/7, very few of us are ever really in the moment. In 2010, there were 3,000 deaths and more than 400,000 injuries due to distracted driving.[2] And more than 1,100 pedestrians went to the emergency room with injuries received while using their cell phones while walking.[3] Being distracted can kill you—and who really wants today to be his or her last day? Get in the moment! I confess to talking while driving or texting while walking. I too have to remind myself to be in the moment! I am encouraging myself as much as I am encouraging you. Live in the now as you drive, jog, or just walk across the street. Not doing so could put you in the hospital! As Ferris Bueller said in the movie *Ferris Bueller's Day Off*, "Life moves pretty fast. If you don't stop and look around once in a while, you could miss it!"

Get in the moment, then do your best to stay there for a while. BE PRESENT, and experience how your true purpose and your true passion rises within you. Now you can really start living a FIRED UP LIFE! Because it's tangible. When we are present, we become capable of hearing the greater, deeper voice within. This requires silence. Be quiet. Don't wait for your turn to talk next. Just listen.

Silence is an activator for all great things, because it requires contemplation and collaboration with something bigger than ourselves—our God, Source, Eternal Energy, love, joy, and inner peace. When we calibrate being present with our inner voice, we not only experience greater happiness, but we get the answers we've been looking for and the solutions to many of our challenges and questions. Being in the moment is powerful and can reap great returns.

So how do we do it? Follow these simple steps in this order and, in my experience, they will work every time.

---

[2] www.distraction.gov.

[3] "Dangers of Distracted Driving Growing," *Daily Herald*, July 31, 2012, www.dailyherald.com/article/20120730/news/707309896/.

FIRED UP and Doing Something About It! Step #7

1. STOP. Just simply stop what you are doing. Think before you speak. You'll sound more intelligent if you do.

2. BREATHE. Feel and be aware of your breath going in and out. This practice is part of Vipassana meditation. Vipassana means seeing things as they really are. Observe your breath for two minutes, and watch how much more present and aware you become.

3. Be in the PRESENT MOMENT. Explore ways of introspection and self-exploration in order to stay in the present—pray, meditate, take a walk, write in a journal, take quiet time for yourself. Be totally focused on whatever you are doing *when you are doing it*. Carefully and slowly move through your daily routine with focus and clarity. Take your time. Chew, enjoy, and taste your food. Do one thing at a time. Turn off your phone when driving. Look at yourself in the mirror and smile. Let peace resonate within you! You are wonderful. Enjoy you, enjoy your life, enjoy what you get to do with it today. BE FIRED UP ABOUT IT!

4. Contemplate the Circle of Life. It's the ultimate paradox, this human condition of ours—birth, life, death. Once you wrap your head around the practice of surrendering yourself to living in the moment, only then will you embrace living a better, more passionate life. The tough part is embracing your flaws and your failures but not letting them define you. Everyone has flaws. It's the realization that you are not the embodiment of your failures that's key. It's knowing that with every failure and challenge you endure, you get closer to living the life you want to live. You learn. You grow. To every season there is a reason. What is your reason to be present today?

The personal growth and learning begins today! When you use the tools in this book, you'll embark on a new path of living a peaceful, fulfilling, and successful life. Thank you for letting me be a part of your journey. I look forward to hearing from you and to remaining FIRED UP with you for life! Post your thoughts, musings, and insights through my social media and/or visit my site at **www.AricBostick.com**. Then go and shout from the rooftops how FIRED UP you are for life! I look forward to hearing from you soon!

Conclusion

Way to go! You did it! Are you FIRED UP? If not, go back and reread the book! It's actually not a bad idea, considering we must saturate our minds with these ideas to the point where they become second nature.

Okay, let's go through the list together. Remember to ask yourself each day:

- What is my FUEL level today?
- What does my INVENTORY look like today? How can I use my strengths today? What should I let go of?
- How can I REFRAME this situation or opportunity today?
- What is my ENERGY plan for today?
- Today I DECLARE that I am… and I will…!
- Who or what needs my UNDERSTANDING today? Can I see his or her point of view?
- Today I will be PRESENT. I will stop to breathe. I will live in the moment!

Are you ready to be FIRED UP for today and for the rest of your life?

Fired Up in Action

These principles really do work. I have used them to overcome just about every obstacle in my life. When I have resisted using them, I have wound up butting my head against the wall until I finally get back to the basics of being FIRED UP! These very principles are the reason I am a speaker today and have had so many wonderful experiences and have formed the amazing relationships in my life.

One of my biggest life lessons came while I was still a full-time school teacher and was trying to organize my own weeklong success and leadership summer camp, called the Camp of CHAMPS. I hired a large marketing firm that charged $50 an hour to help me plan and promote my camp. Before I launched Camp of CHAMPS, I had held two small camps in a high school cafeteria and a church multi-purpose center. The first camp had 75 students and the other had 60 students. The marketing firm and I rented out the Zaragoza Theater at Six Flags San Antonio, which has a seating capacity for 1,500. We made television and radio commercials and printed 15,000 brochures. Here I was a school teacher making $31,000 a year, I was nearly $30,000 in credit card debt, and I had the nerve to hire this firm and book this large venue for a camp that I had no idea that anybody would sign up for. I had only done about 20 professional presentations at the time; I had no credibility and no one knew who I was. To say I did not have any sort of following or name recognition would be putting it lightly.

When I had signed up only 35 students and received the bill from the marketing firm for several thousand dollars for a camp with minimal attendance, I was definitely NOT FIRED UP! I was feeling badly burned! I had two choices: Quit and blame the marketing company and never try again, or remember why I wanted to put on this camp in the first place.

What was my FUEL? Why hold a success and leadership camp for middle- and high-school students? I had three reasons. One: How great would it be to learn the principles of success for living as a teen rather than in your mid-thirties? Two: I wanted young people to know that they can and will overcome their present circumstances and hardships if they let go of the past, set goals and take action on them, and start to think of others more than themselves. Three: A coach, a teacher, and a counselor taught this to me and it changed my life. I had the ability to share and pass this knowledge and these skills onto others.

I took INVENTORY of my situation. I realized I needed to become a full-time speaker, I needed to create relationships with school sponsors and leadership educators around the state, and I needed to make this wrong right. I negotiated a year reprieve on my contract with Six Flags. I personally called all 35 families who signed up their children for Camp of CHAMPS and told them I was refunding their money with the hope that they would sign up again for next year's camp. Which would absolutely happen!

I commenced to REFRAMING my attitude and said this camp was not meant to be at this time. I wasn't ready; I lacked experience and I didn't have enough team support around me. I ENERGIZED myself by taking better care of myself and balancing my life once again—physically, financially, and spiritually. Finally, I DECLARED my goals, **"I will become a full-time speaker and I will have a successful summer camp a year from this date!"**

Then I did something I had never really done before. I surrendered my goal to God. I said, "God, you know what I want, but You know better than I do. I will wash toilets, mow lawns, or teach school for the rest of my life. I just want to do Your will. Thy will be done." I realized that I was forcing order, trying to make things happen rather than letting them happen. A power bigger than me had to run the show from there on out. For me that power is God, and I had to let go and get out of the way.

But I also believe God helps those who help themselves. I had to do my part. Goals and dreams don't just happen. It has been said that success is the place where opportunity and preparation meet. Thus, I had to do the work. I realized I couldn't just leave it up to a marketing company and television and radio commercials to get students to sign up. I had to go about the hard work of building relationships with students and the educators and parents who lead them.

I had spoken for an organization that held leadership camps and trainings and was contracted to do their summer camp a week after mine. My camp had just failed so I put all my energy into preparing for their camp. I FIRED UP their camp counselors, the students, even the educators through the workshops and keynote presentation I did that week. I was so well received that many of the educators wanted to contract me to speak at their schools! The organization hosting the camp offered me a year-long contract to speak at all of their events for the next 12 months! For the next year, I would be presenting to students and the educators—from all over Texas—who hire speakers! I was allowed to promote my summer camp at these events and—wouldn't you know it—with no radio commercial, no television commercial, no expensive marketing firm, and only 4,000 brochures distributed, 300 students signed up to attend my camp the very next summer. I made good on my contract with Six Flags, settled my bill with the marketing company, and to date have held camps for more than a decade all over the country! Thousands of students have been inspired!

A full year after my failed camp, I came to UNDERSTAND what success truly is. The epiphany happened to me on the second day of Camp of CHAMPS. The first day went well, but I really was just in survival mode speaking and managing this enormous event. I tried to be genuine but I had a hard time identifying individual students from the sea of 300 faces of kids from all over Texas.

Two students who had signed up the year before—and whose money I had refunded because we cancelled—had signed up again to attend camp. One of my staff grabbed me that second morning and said, "AJ's mom is here and she is demanding to speak to you." I rushed out and greeted the mother and said, "Hi Mrs. Flores, how can I help you? Is everything ok with AJ?" She said, "I don't know what you have done to my son!" I said, "What happened?" She told me, "AJ came home last night and cleaned his room for the first time in months! He said, 'Aric said you have to set goals, take action, listen to your parents, and be your best! I am going to change my life starting right now, Mom!'" I was speechless.

AJ Flores and his peer John Elizondo were in the seventh grade when they came to camp that year. They attended camp each summer until their junior year in college! They come from amazing families with super parents who encouraged their kids to be their best. I taught them to set goals and believe in themselves. Both had great high school careers academically and achieved in sports and band respectively. They both graduated from college. AJ is excelling in the corporate world and John, who set a goal in seventh grade to become a sports broadcaster, is now a 22-year-old newscaster in Waco, Texas.

So it turns out that these principles really work! If I had given up on my goals to be a full-time speaker and hold success and leadership camps for young people, then I would have missed out on being a part of these two amazing young men's lives. I believe they would have been successful without me, but I sure feel good about my contribution to their success. But I had to let go of the past and live in the PRESENT so I could move forward and accomplish the goals I had set for myself.

The point is, the same goes for you. Stop looking back! Quit worrying about tomorrow! LIVE NOW AND GO FOR IT! You are not burned out unless you decide to extinguish your flame. GET FIRED UP FOR YOUR SUCCESSFUL LIFE! You define your success! Decide now who you are going to be, what you really want to do, take action, and leave the rest up to a power greater than yourself. I promise it will all work out just how it is supposed to. J.K. Rowling said, "Everything that fails brings you closer to what works." She experienced hardship and failure before Harry Potter became a worldwide sensation!

So what are you waiting for? Get FIRED UP and start climbing! Zig Ziglar titled one of his books *See You at the Top*. I believed him then and I believe him now. I'll be seeing you at the top, my friend.

Let's Continue This Journey Together at www.AricBostick.com!
Be sure to visit my website at www.AricBostick.com today! You can join my FIRED UP SUCCESS TEAM to receive my video messages as well as other success tools! And also please join my AricBostick Fanpage, and follow me on Twitter, Pinterest, Instagram, YouTube, and LinkedIn for regular doses of inspiration and to stay updated on what the Fired Up Team is creating to help you keep your fire lit!

Want to Hear Me Speak?
If you would like to have me speak at your next event or see what kind of training I do, please visit my site at www.AricBostick.com or call our team at 1-888-629-0179.

Notes

Notes

Notes

Notes